MW01515821

HowExpert Presents

How To Buy a Car

Your Step By Step Guide In Buying a Car

HowExpert

For more tips related to this topic, visit HowExpert.com/buycar.

Recommended Resources

- HowExpert.com – Quick 'How To' Guides on All Topics from A to Z by Everyday Experts.
- HowExpert.com/free – Free HowExpert Email Newsletter.
- HowExpert.com/books – HowExpert Books
- HowExpert.com/courses – HowExpert Courses
- HowExpert.com/clothing – HowExpert Clothing
- HowExpert.com/membership – HowExpert Membership Site
- HowExpert.com/affiliates – HowExpert Affiliate Program
- HowExpert.com/writers – Write About Your #1 Passion/Knowledge/Expertise & Become a HowExpert Author.
- HowExpert.com/resources – Additional HowExpert Recommended Resources
- YouTube.com/HowExpert – Subscribe to HowExpert YouTube.
- Instagram.com/HowExpert – Follow HowExpert on Instagram.
- Facebook.com/HowExpert – Follow HowExpert on Facebook.

Publisher's Foreword

Dear HowExpert reader,

HowExpert publishes quick 'how to' guides on all topics from A to Z by everyday experts.

At HowExpert, our mission is to discover, empower, and maximize talents of everyday people to ultimately make a positive impact in the world for all topics from A to Z...one everyday expert at a time!

All of our HowExpert guides are written by everyday people just like you and me who have a passion, knowledge, and expertise for a specific topic.

We take great pride in selecting everyday experts who have a passion, great writing skills, and knowledge about a topic that they love to be able to teach you about the topic you are also passionate about and eager to learn about.

We hope you get a lot of value from our HowExpert guides and it can make a positive impact in your life in some kind of way. All of our readers including you altogether help us continue living our mission of making a positive impact in the world for all spheres of influences from A to Z.

If you enjoyed one of our HowExpert guides, then please take a moment to send us your feedback from wherever you got this book.

Thank you and we wish you all the best in all aspects of life.

Sincerely,

BJ Min
Founder & Publisher of HowExpert
HowExpert.com

PS...If you are also interested in becoming a HowExpert author, then please visit our website at HowExpert.com/writers. Thank you & again, all the best!

Table of Contents

Recommended Resources 2

Publisher's Foreword 3

Introduction 8

Chapter 1: How to Choose the Right Vehicle
Check List: 9

What is My Budget? 9

What Do You Need the Car For? 9

What are the Running Costs? 10

Can I Afford to Fix Problems? 10

What is the Reliability Reputation? 11

What is the Service Reputation of the Dealers? 11

Chapter 2: How to Get the Best Price for Your
Trade-In 12

Trade-In Checklist: 12

20-Point Checklist to Check a Used Car 13

How to Check Service History 16

**Chapter 3: How to Not Get Ripped Off During
Financing** **18**

Five Types Of Finance Options: *18*

Straightforward Hire Purchase 18

PCP Finance (Personal Contract Purchase) or
Guaranteed Future Value Finance 19

Balloon Payments 20

Contract Hire / Leasing 21

Negative Equity Loans 22

**Chapter 4: How to Guide on Insurance
Products** **23**

Guaranteed Asset Protection *23*

Payment Protection *24*

Warranty *25*

Chapter 5: Paint Protection Explained 27

Chapter 6: How to Spot Fleet Cars and Ex-Rentals.. 28

Exceptions: 29

Chapter 7: Tips When Walking into a Dealership 30

The Sales Department Dealership Hierarchy 31

Chapter 8: Common Lies............................. 32

Chapter 9: The Insider's Sales Process Revealed 33

Final Words 36

Recommended Resources 37

Introduction

Most people feel intimidated at the prospect of walking into a car dealership and purchasing a new or used vehicle. This is because dealerships have a reputation of ripping people off.

This guide will tell you some of the secrets and show you how to go about buying a car.

So, you are in the market for a new car. Maybe this is your first vehicle purchase or maybe it is your tenth. It doesn't matter, but you should still follow these tips to help you get a good deal.

- The first thing you have to do is choose what car you want to buy. This may be obvious, but many people walk into a dealership without a clue.

- You may be thinking, "It's the salesman job to sell me one." Yes, you are correct, but this also means you are not educated on specs, prices, residual values, insurance prices, so on and so forth.

- Start your research on the Internet. It will provide you with all the information you will need. Reviews, prices, insurance quotes, trade in values, and much more can be found here.

Chapter 1: How to Choose the Right Vehicle Check List:

What is My Budget?

- How much you want to spend on the car?
  - o This is the first thing you must decide. Look at your finances and calculate how much you can afford and do not overshoot your budget.
- How much you can afford to pay monthly?
  - o Now you know how much you can afford, consider the cost on a monthly basis. Do some research on the prices so you get an idea of the average amount of money you need to borrow.

What Do You Need the Car For?

- Family
  - o Take into consideration what size family you have and whether you plan to extend it in the near future.

- Check safety standards and storage space, usability and try a few models out.
- Work
  - Make sure it fits into your working life, so if you drive a lot make sure the car is comfortable and has excellent fuel economy.

What are the Running Costs?

- Servicing
- Gas
- Consumables (such a tires)
- Insurance
- Tax

Can I Afford to Fix Problems?

- Check the price of parts because, depending on the model and manufacturer, some can be very expensive.

What is the Reliability Reputation?

- If the manufacturer has a poor record or that particular car has a bad reputation, you may find yourself at the garage every couple of months – or worse.

What is the Service Reputation of the Dealers?

- Some car dealers have the worst customer service. It is a good idea to check reviews before you buy a car from them to know what kind of business you'll be doing.

Chapter 2: How to Get the Best Price for Your Trade-In

The trade in is the worst part of the deal for both the salesman and the new-car buyer. Both want a certain price, and often they are far apart.

The best thing to do is to find out from a reputable source (like Kelley Blue Book) what the trade-in value of your car is. Take into account the condition and mileage of your vehicle. Be honest with yourself.

Don't have any unrealistic numbers in your head. The importance of knowing the true value of your car is to keep from getting ripped off by an unscrupulous salesman's undervaluation.

Black Book USA, Black Book UK, Glasses Guide UK, and Kelley Blue Book are good places to start to find out the value of your vehicle.

Trade-In Checklist:

- Vehicle ownership documents
- Service history
- Any bills relating to maintenance
- All keys
- Finance papers

Any other documents or history of the car will also be useful when getting a good price.

20-Point Checklist to Check a Used Car

Here is a 20-point checklist everyone should use when buying a used car.

1. Take a quick walk around the car maybe twice; get familiar with the lines of the car.

2. Have a look at the paint in the light, stand back and check the colour of each panel. This is to check for light-impact damage. If any area looks slightly lighter or darker, chances are good that it has been painted.

3. Now walk around again and take a look where all the panels meet. Make sure all of the gaps are even. This is to check for any hard-impact damage.

4. Check for overspray around the lights, windowsills and wheel arches.

5. Look at the middle of the roof inside and out, and beneath of the chassis. You are looking for

creases and signs of welding to see it the car is a cut and shut (two different cars put together).

6. Lift the hood and check the front beam for any signs of new paint in order to see if there has been any front-end impact.

7. Next walk around the car tapping the panels to check for filler.

8. By looking at the body from various angles you should be able to see dents and scratches on the surface of the car.

9. Now walk around the car and check all of the tires. Look for any bulges or uneven wear. A new set of front tires can set you back hundreds and sometimes thousands of dollars.

10. Grab each wheel with both hands and try and move it by pulling and pushing hard. If there is play in the wheel it can be very expensive to repair. Anything from a wheel bearing or CV joint can be broken. Walk around and press on each corner of the car checking the suspension for any creaking.

11. As you go around doing this, check the brake discs for wear, if you can feel a large lip around the edges it means they will need replacing.

12. Open the bonnet and check the oil, brake fluid, and radiator levels. Unscrew the oil cap and look for dark green gunk. This means that the head gasket is on the way out. Now start the car up and listen for any strange noises or sounds.

13. Take a look inside the radiator again and see if there are any bubbles. That could mean that the head of the engine is cracked.

14. Now, get in the car and play with every single button you see. This is to check that everything is working. Put the lights on, the indicators, everything.

15. Take the car for a long drive and make sure it feels smooth and all the gears work. If it is an automatic, put your foot down on the gas and accelerate hard to see how the car reacts.

16. Test to see if the brakes work to your satisfaction; if the car has ABS (antilock braking system), test to make sure it works.

17. Check all the paperwork. The car should have a full-service history backed up with bills and receipts. Look for main dealer stamps and what kind of work has been carried out.

18. Most importantly, check when the timing belts were changed. Most garages will put a sticker on the engine to tell you when the work was done. If you are not sure, you may need to do this yourself, because it is very important to the wellbeing of you and your car. If the belts have not been changed, then any one of them could snap at any time and the pistons could fire through the top of the engine, thus ending its life.

19. Make sure the owner on the registration documents is the person selling the car; check their ID.

20. If you are happy with everything, go ahead with your purchase. Use anything that you have found on this list as a bargaining tool. You will have to pay to put things right.

How to Check Service History

When buying a used car, it is very important to check that the car has a full-service history from a reputable garage.

During the first three years, all work should have been carried out by the franchise dealer. Any work after the first three years should have been done by a specialist or certified garage.

It is important that you find out what the service schedules are for the car. Don't take the salesman's word.

Chapter 3: How to Not Get Ripped Off During Financing

When it comes down to setting up the finance plan, you will meet with someone who is called a business manager. Their job is to sell the loan and all of its add-ons.

Five Types Of Finance Options:

Straightforward Hire Purchase

- You will put a deposit down on the car and pay the balance monthly for a period of time before the car will be yours.

- This is the most common way of owning a car and is very easy to understand.

- Be careful that you get a good rate and that the period of time you will pay isn't stretched out longer to make the payments smaller but keep your paying interest.

- Always ask for the interest rate and then add all the payments up over a fixed period of time to figure out your total cost.

PCP Finance (Personal Contract Purchase) or Guaranteed Future Value Finance

- This is a great way to buy a car if you like to change it up every two or three years.

- This type of finance lets you keep the monthly payments low and to a short period of time.

- It works by setting the future value of the car; this is given by the manufacturer as they will be buying the car back of you.

- This means a large proportion of the amount that you finance will not be included, usually up to 35%. So, you will put down a deposit of around 10% to 20% and finance the remainder.

- The best deals to be had are the advertised ones where they are promoting a new car and the rate and payments are shown nationally.

- The problem with this is that many business mangers see the payments will be lower so they raise the interest rate by up to 50% higher than usual.

- This gives a larger profit and greater commission.

- This is so if the value of the car drops considerably, the future value is guaranteed by the dealer.

- They will have to buy the car back at the agreed price no matter what the value is.

- Also be careful as the value set is calculated on your annual mileage.

- If you do more you will be hit with penalties for each additional mile.

Balloon Payments

- This type of payment is not recommended for private buyers, a lot of people in the USA and UK fell into this trap many years ago when it was first introduced.

- What happens is, say you want to borrow a certain amount but can only afford to pay a small monthly payment. The business manager defers an amount by up to 60%, therefore giving you a lower monthly payment.

- The catch is that this payment must be paid at the end of the term.
- As we know, cars lose value fast, so people found themselves owing more than what the car was worth.
- This meant taking out an extra loan to pay off the difference.

Contract Hire / Leasing

- This form of finance is for people who never want to own the car but prefer to lease for a period of time.
- For this type of finance, remember the mileage is set per year and if you go over, penalties will be incurred.
- Also make sure to find out whether servicing is included or not.
- You cannot end the lease early. If you do, you will pay fines.

Negative Equity Loans

- NELs are for people who owe for more than their car and are added onto the car loan.

- If you are in this situation, it is a good idea not to buy an expensive car.

- All you are doing is getting yourself into more debt.

- Try going for a personal bank loan and buy the new car with that money.

Chapter 4: How to Guide on Insurance Products

Guaranteed Asset Protection

- What this type of insurance does is act as a top up between your car insurance and the retail value of your vehicle.

- When you drive off in your car, the value of it begins to decline.

- If your vehicle is in an accident or is stolen, the value you will receive will be less than what you paid for it.

- What this product will do fill the gap between what your insurance company offers you so there will be no negotiation over the settlement price.

- Two checks will arrive in the post and you simply go a buy a new car.

- It is valid only for the first three years of ownership and cannot be renewed.

- If you have bought your car on finance than this type of insurance is extremely important and highly recommended.

- Imagine you have bought a car for $10,000 on finance. One year down the line you have an accident and need a new car.

- The insurance company offers you $7,000 for the car and you still owe $8,500.

- When you go to find a one-year-old example from a dealer you find that they are selling them for $8,750 so you will have to come up with more money to buy the car.

- GAP fixes this so you walk into the showroom and buy a new car with no problems.

- Dealers tend to charge high prices. For the best deals ask your own insurance company or search on the internet.

Payment Protection

- This type of insurance is the most commonly sold product when it comes to borrowing money.

- The terms are never explained and often the insurance never pays out.

- This is because in the terms and conditions there are so many clauses that it is very hard to make a successful claim.

- Customers are either told they must take it to get the finance or are sold it with promises it does not deliver.

- Although there have been more regulations in this market it is still pushed on to consumers who do not need it.

- The best advice is to check the fine print and read all the terms.

Warranty

- A warranty is something that is provided as insurance cover on mechanical failure on a car.

- All new cars will come with at least three years coverage. If you are buying a used car then the most dealers will only offer a few months or a year and try to get you to buy an extended warranty.

- Dealer warranties are the best. These usually cover most parts and situations. Be careful with other warranties as they do not cover wear and tear.

Chapter 5: Paint Protection Explained

At some stage, usually at the end or during the finance selling, you will be offered interior and paint protection.

They do work if applied to your car in the proper way. This is seldom done as they are looking to get as many cars done in a day to receive a bonus.

The actual kits will cost around a fifth of the price that they are offered to you for so the mark up is very high.

At cost price plus labor, the product is well worth it, but at the price you will be charged, it is probably a good idea to steer clear. If you want this type of protection, go to a professional car cleaner and you will receive a quality finish at a cheaper price.

Chapter 6: How to Spot Fleet Cars and Ex-Rentals

- Buying used cars can be hit or miss. Going to a car dealer is a safer bet over a person on the street.

- There are a few things to look out for when purchasing a used car from a dealer.

- Most of the cars that are three- to six-months old and have about 6,000 to 14,000 miles on them are fleet cars.

- The term fleet car means basically that the company that bought them purchased more than one car (probably more than fifty).

- The biggest portions of these cars are actually ex-rentals, though the salesman will tell you otherwise.

- They will tell you these are ex-company cars or manager's cars.

- As we all know, rental cars are not looked after and most have been driven very hard.

- The two most popular rental companies that provide to the trade are "Enterprise Rent A

Car" and "AVIS Car Rentals" both will use and abbreviated name on the vehicle registration documents to hide the true origin of the vehicle, for example Enterprise use "ERAC" on the documents.

Unless you are happy with buying an ex-rental vehicle, stay away from six-month-old cars.

Exceptions:

Some exceptions include ex-demo vehicles that have been owned by the dealership or company (check registration documents for proof).

Pre-registered cars are also ok to buy. A pre-registered car is when a dealer has not met their target of cars sold and therefore has to register the number of cars so that they get their bonus from the manufacturer.

Don't forget that although these cars are brand new the three-year warranty has already started on the date of it being registered.

Chapter 7: Tips When Walking into a Dealership

When you are going to a car dealership, there are a few pointers that you need to follow so that you don't fall into the hands of the sales man.

- First, when you are looking for a used car, you will probably search all the car dealers in your area to find the exact model, year, and price then phone up and take a look at the car.

- This is the wrong thing to do. Yes, search for your ideal car and phone up to see if it's available, even better to email them.

- When you enter the car lot, DO NOT walk straight up to the car you want to buy. The salesman will see this and know that is the car you want. This will give him the edge.

- Instead, take a casual walk around and don't pay any attention to the car. Wait until someone approaches you then have that person sit with you and take you through the sales process.

- This will give them the feeling they are in control. Give them a rough idea of what you are looking for and then let the salesman show you some cars.

- Do not show too much interest in the car you came to see but slowly edge towards that one as the one that interests you the most.
- The point you are trying to make is that if the salesman doesn't give you the deal you are after then there are many others cars out there that you will look at and buy.

The Sales Department Dealership Hierarchy

- General Manager
- Sales Manager
- Business Manager
- Sales Executives

Chapter 8: Common Lies

- This is the manager's wife car
- This is an ex-company car that has been cared for
- You cannot buy these cars new anymore
- There's a waiting list for these cars
- The car will not depreciate like others
- I have someone else coming to see the car today
- If you take the payment protection insurance, we can guarantee you finance
- The warranty covers everything

Chapter 9: The Insider's Sales Process Revealed

- When you buy a car from a dealer, they will have trained their staff to follow a sales process.

- This is to ensure the maximum amount of sales.

- What the salesman will be taught is a strict process that they must adhere to.

- The process will be closely monitored by the manager to make sure the price is maximized.

- As soon as you walk into a dealership, watch to see how the dealer will try to control you, the customer, and put you in a position where you feel you must buy.

- To recap, what they are trying to do first is find out what car you drive at the moment and what you are looking to buy next.

- A lot of salespeople will try to find out what price you want for your car or if you have had any quotes already.

- This is an underhanded technique so they can give you less for your car or play with the figures to make it look like you are getting a good deal.

- One common tactic is to find out over the phone or find a car in stock. This is so that you do not know about the price of the car.

- Now they can inflate the price and either give you a large discount or more for your car.

- Really all they have done is made up some figures and the invoice will still be written with their own figures in it.

- Now they will find the car and make sure it's the one you want to buy. Once they have confirmed this then they will take you on a test drive.

- Only after this will they start talking about the price of the car, the reason for this is because they have manufactured your desire.

- This is common practice with husband and wife buyers, they feel that they don't want to lose the car.

- Then they will give you the price of your car and negotiate the deal.

Please bear in mind that the car will probably be sold to a trade buyer who has good ties with the manager and both will make a lot of money out of the deal.

Final Words

Use these insider tips when you purchase your next car. At least you will be aware of what goes on and what to look for.

Being educated in all the products and services is important as many people find that they end up with stuff they don't want or are in financial difficulty because of the type of finance they were advised to get.

Getting out of trouble when making a wrong purchase will always cost the buyer a lot of money – so just remember to play it safe and if it is too good to be true, then it probably really is.

Recommended Resources

- <u>HowExpert.com</u> – Quick 'How To' Guides on All Topics from A to Z by Everyday Experts.
- <u>HowExpert.com/free</u> – Free HowExpert Email Newsletter.
- <u>HowExpert.com/books</u> – HowExpert Books
- <u>HowExpert.com/courses</u> – HowExpert Courses
- <u>HowExpert.com/clothing</u> – HowExpert Clothing
- <u>HowExpert.com/membership</u> – HowExpert Membership Site
- <u>HowExpert.com/affiliates</u> – HowExpert Affiliate Program
- <u>HowExpert.com/writers</u> – Write About Your #1 Passion/Knowledge/Expertise & Become a HowExpert Author.
- <u>HowExpert.com/resources</u> – Additional HowExpert Recommended Resources
- <u>YouTube.com/HowExpert</u> – Subscribe to HowExpert YouTube.
- <u>Instagram.com/HowExpert</u> – Follow HowExpert on Instagram.
- <u>Facebook.com/HowExpert</u> – Follow HowExpert on Facebook.